Anonymous

A Church Manual

Anonymous

A Church Manual

ISBN/EAN: 9783744694070

Printed in Europe, USA, Canada, Australia, Japan

Cover: Foto ©Lupo / pixelio.de

More available books at **www.hansebooks.com**

A

CHURCH MANUAL;

WITH

BRIEF HISTORICAL NOTICES

OF THE

FIRST CONGREGATIONAL CHURCH

IN BRAINTREE,

AND ITS PASTORS,

FROM THE DATE OF ITS ORGANIZATION, TILL THE

CLOSE OF 1859.

PUBLISHED BY ORDER OF THE CHURCH.

BOSTON:

HAYDEN & RANDALL, 23 CORNHILL.

1860.

BRIEF HISTORICAL NOTICES

First Congregational Church in Braintree.

THE *original* "Church of Braintree," known as the "First Congregational Church of Quincy," was gathered September 17, 1639. Braintree then included the whole territory now divided between the present incorporated towns of Quincy, Braintree, and Randolph.

What is now known as the "First Congregational Church of Braintree," was organized September 10, 1707. Of the causes operating to its separation from the mother church, we have little or no information except what is derived from "two discourses" of Rev. Mr. Lunt, late pastor of the Quincy Church, delivered September 29, 1839, on the two hundredth anniversary of its gathering. From the "appendices" and notes illustrating these discourses, we learn that as early as January, 1704-5, "two church meetings were held that occasioned much debate, and some misapprehension about church discipline;"—that "nine of the church withdrew from the Lord's table, and in many things acted disorderly;" and that difficulties and dissensions were so great, as to render necessary the calling of a council of Elders and Messengers. This council met, May 7, 1707.

Previous to this date however — as early as May 2, 1706, "a new house was raised in Braintree for a meeting-house;" of course a secession from the "original" church had been determined on; this was more than two years before the seceders became recognized by civil authority, as forming a distinct precinct. The reasons assigned for this movement, were briefly — that the old meeting-house was not large enough to accommodate "above two-thirds of the inhabitants;"— that "its position was near one end of the town,

and of inconvenient access to half the population ; "— that
" for near a dozen years, they had petitioned in vain for a
larger and more central house ; " and that in their judgment,
no alternative remained but to establish separate worship,
and maintain it as God should enable them to do. Whether
for good or ill, it is clear that the mantle of the father's logic
has not been cast away by the children.

The alienation between the mother and daughter churches,
seems to have continued some two years ; when, agreeably to
" the advice of ministers for reconciliation," " the acknowl-
edgment of haste and irregularity " on the part of the daughter
church, was made to the mother church, Feb. 19, 1709–10 ;
a month later, Rev. Mr. Adams preached in the old meeting-
house, in token of mutual forgiveness and forgetfulness of
past offences.

Rev. Hugh Adams, who had graduated at Harvard University in 1676, was ordained first pastor of the newly organized
church, on the 10th of September, the same day on which
the organization took place.°

The sermon, on occasion of the church's organization, was
preached by Rev. Cotton Mather, of Boston, from Eph. 2 : 22,
" In whom ye also are builded together,"—from which the
doctrine was deduced, that " Every particular church of the
Lord Jesus Christ, is to be together built in the glorious Lord
as a temple of God." In applying the subject to the members
of the newly constituted church, he says :

" Brethren ! 'tis a very great glory which is this day put
upon you by this Glorious One ! But as you must beware of
being haughty, because you now stand in the Lord's holy
mountain, so your standing there should make you very cau-
tious, very watchful, that your whole behavior may adorn the
doctrine of God your Savior. You have the eyes of the most
Holy Lord upon you — eyes that strike and pierce like lightning — pure eyes that cannot look upon iniquity ! The people
of God, and all your neighbors have their eyes upon you !

° From the Parish records of Braintree. It appears that Mr. A. failed to realize his
wishes in the matter of pecuniary support from the people, and complained to the
"General Court" of ill usage in that respect, without obtaining redress. While at
Durham, he made similar complaint to the "Provincial Assembly" of N. H., of the
delinquency and trespasses of his parishioners — praying not only for justice to
himself, but that a neglect to pay a minister might be made penal and presentable
by the "grand jury." These, and other facts not necessary to be repeated, led
Dr. Belknap (Hist. Colls. II. 305) to pronounce him "one of the most eccentric
clergymen ever settled in N. H."

O how much ought this to be your prayer — ' Teach me thy way. O Lord, and lead me in a plain path !' It is equally to be desired — greatly to be *advised* — that you endeavor greatly to approve yourselves the children of God, without rebuke, in the midst of those who may be ready eno' to condemn you — that you may keep close to the faith and order of the gospel, and the right way of the Lord — that you may be much in supplications to the Lord, and often set apart whole days for extraordinary supplication, that the work of God may be happily carried on among you ; — in a word, that you may all be true citizens of Zion ! This is greatly to be desired ! "

The discourse closes thus :

" May this church be such a temple; then, as there were cherubims on the walls of the temple, the very angels of God will take pleasure to behold you, to befriend you ; yea, then the Glorious Lord himself will afford a most gracious presence of His to you ! And, Lord ! if thou will be here, we shall not die, nor shall the souls of our children die ! The name of this church will be, Jehovah Shammah—the Lord is there ! "

The covenant upon which the church was originally gathered, is found appended to Rev. Mr. Mather's sermon, preached at its organization — and is there noticed, "as a perpetual monitor of the flock, to be steadfast in the covenant, *in perpetuam rei memoriam.*"

" We, whose names are hereunto subscribed, apprehending ourselves called of God, to join together in church communion, (acknowledging our unworthiness of such a privilege, and our inability to keep covenant with God, or to perform any spiritual duty, unless Christ shall enable us thereto,) in humble dependence on free grace for divine assistance and acceptance ; we do, in the name of Jesus Christ our Lord, fully covenant and bind ourselves, solemnly, in the presence of God himself — His holy angels, and all His servants here present, to serve the God whose name alone is Jehovah, Father, Son, and Holy Ghost, the only true and living God, cleaving to Him as our chief good ; and unto our Lord Jesus Christ, as our only Savior, prophet, priest, and king of our souls, in a way of gospel obedience ; avouching the Lord to be our God, and the God of our children, whom we give unto Him ; counting it as a high favor, that the Lord will accept

1*

of us and our children with us, to be His people. We do
also give ourselves one unto another in the Lord, covenanting
to walk together as a church of Christ, in all the ways of his
worship, according to the holy rules of his word, promising
in brotherly love, faithfully to watch over one another's souls,
and to submit ourselves to the discipline and power of Christ
in his church ; and duly to attend the seals and censures, or
whatever ordinances Christ has commanded to be observed by
his people, so far as the Lord, by his word and Spirit, has or
shall reveal unto us to be our duty ; beseeching the Lord to
own us for his people, and to delight to dwell in the midst
of us.

   " And, that we may keep our covenants with God, we desire
to deny ourselves, and to depend wholly on the free mercy of
God, and upon the merits of Jesus Christ; and wherein we
shall fail, to wait on him for pardon, thro' his name ; beseeching the Lord to own us as a church of Christ, and to delight
to abide in the midst of us."

   The following " covenant " appears on the records, without
date or name ; whether adopted in the days of Mr. Niles,
or Mr. Weld, we have not the means of ascertaining.   Its
greater *particularity* chiefly distinguishes it from the foregoing :

CHURCH COVENANT.

   We do at this time, and in the name of our Lord Jesus Christ, and in
dependence on the influence of his Holy Spirit, enter into covenant with
God and one another according to the following words:—

   I.   That having chosen the Lord Jehovah to be our God, we will fear
and cleave unto him in love, and serve him in truth with all our hearts,
giving up ourselves to him to be his people, to be at his direction and
disposal in all things, that we may enjoy and hold communion with him,
as members of Christ's mystical body, according to his revealed will, to
the end of our lives.

   II.   We promise to keep close to the truth of Christ, endeavoring with
lively affection toward it, to defend it against all opposers ; and that we
may do this, we resolve to use the Holy Scriptures, as our rule and platform to walk by ; by which we may discern the mind of Christ, and not
be led away and entangled with the unscriptural inventions of men.

   III.   We oblige ourselves to the faithful improvement of our abilities
and opportunities, to worship God, according to all the institutions of
Jesus Christ, taking the great Emmanuel to be our Savior, in all his
offices ; endeavoring with the help of God to give reverend attention to
the word of God, to pray to, and to praise him, to hold communion with
each other, in the observation of all the holy institutions of Christ, which
he hath established for his Church under the gospel, especially in both the
seals of the covenant of grace, viz: Baptism, and the Lord's Supper.

IV. We engage, with the Lord's help, to have a careful inspection over our hearts, so as to endeavor, by the virtue of the death of Christ, the mortification of all our sinful passions, worldly frames, and irregular affections; to abstain from all open and scandalous sins, by which the enemies of our holy religion may be encouraged to blaspheme the blessed Jesus, and from all secret and private sins, by which we shall depart from the living God.

V. We promise, with the help of God, to maintain the worship of God in our families, evening and morning; to read the scriptures to them, and to pray with them; to bring up our children in the nurture and admonition of the Lord; to instruct them, and all under our care, in the knowledge and fear of God, according to our best abilities, particularly by the use of the Orthodox Catechism of the Assembly of Divines, the truths of which we profess; that so, true religion may be maintained and known by our families, while we live; and that our posterity may know and fear the Lord and obey the living and true God aright, and adhere to his truths when we are dead.

VI. We promise that we will peaceably submit to the holy discipline, appointed by Christ in his Church for offenders, obeying them who have the rule over us in the Lord; and will endeavor to maintain a holy orthodox ministry among us in this place.

VII. We bind ourselves to walk in love, one toward another, endeavoring our mutual edification; visiting, exhorting, and comforting, as occasion may be, our brother or sister that offendeth; not divulging private offences irregularly, but carefully following the several precepts laid down by Christ in the gospel for church discipline, willingly forgiving all who manifest to a judgment of charity that they truly repent.

VIII. We will endeavor with the help of God, to govern and regulate ourselves, in the management of church discipline, according to the advice and direction given us in the word of God, and we trust according to the method of the Congregational Churches in this land, of which particular denomination we publicly profess ourselves, standing in a near and sisterly relation to all such Churches of Christ, and desirous to maintain all special acts of communion with them, which the communion of saints allows and requires, according to the Platform of Church Discipline agreed upon by the elders and messengers of the Churches in the year 1648, at Cambridge, in New England.

IX. And now we beseech God, who is witness to this our covenant transaction between him and us, and one another, to enable us to keep this covenant inviolably to his glory and to our own edification and salvation. And that wherein we shall fail of obedience, he may give us repentance, pardon and healing, for the sake of our Lord Jesus Christ. AMEN.

Through disagreement with his people on the subject of salary, Mr. Adams relinquished his charge, August 22, 1710, having held it less than three years. He was next settled at Chatham, but took his dismission April 25, 1716; afterwards he was installed in Durham, N. H., March, 1718, and there labored in the ministry till January, 1739, when he was dismissed, though he lived till 1750, and died at the age of 74.

After the dismission of Mr. Adams, several candidates were employed on probation, through nine succeeding months; from among these, Mr. Samuel Niles was chosen to the vacant office, by a vote of great, though not entire, unanimity. His ordination occurred May 23, 1711, when the sermon on the occasion was delivered by the pastor elect, agreeably to the usage of those days, from Romans 15:30—"Strive together with me in your prayers to God for me." In behalf of the Council he was introduced to the communion of the church by Rev. Joseph Belcher, of Dedham; the charge was given by Rev. Peter Thatcher, of Milton; the right hand of fellowship, by Rev. John Danforth, of Dorchester; and the imposition of hands in the consecration service, by Rev. Messrs. Thatcher, of Milton, Danforth, Belcher, and Thatcher, of Weymouth. The council, though small compared with similar bodies in later times, was sufficiently "venerable," as viewed from the stand-point of 1860, and probably embraced all the then existing "neighbor churches" and pastors of unquestioned orthodoxy.

In this connection it is pertinent to say—that Rev. Mr. Niles was born at Block-Island, May 1, 1674, and graduated at Harvard University, in 1699. After leaving college, and preparing himself for the sacred vocation he had chosen, he commenced preaching in a district of Rhode Island, then called "ministerial lands,"—now known as South Kingston; it does not appear that he had there a pastoral charge, but labored as a missionary, or "stated supply," for several years. His life and labors closed in Braintree, May 1, 1762, being then eighty-eight years of age, to a day, and having continued his public services down to the last sabbath preceding his death.*

---

* It may not be out of place to record here a few additional facts concerning this able and devoted servant of God for which we are chiefly indebted to the kindness of Rev. J. B. Felt. He himself records the place of his nativity, as above, in his "Manuscript History of the Indian and French Wars;" "he was a descendant, most probably a grandson of John Niles, who was of Braintree from 1639 to his decease in February, 1696, aged 94, and had sons. John, Joseph, Nathaniel, Samuel, Increase, Benjamin and Isaac." From which of these sons he descended is not clear. His first wife was daughter of Rev. Peter Thatcher, of Milton, and died in 1716. His second wife was Ann Coddington, who died 1732. Rev. Mr. Niles published "Tristia Ecclesiarum" or, "A sorrowful account of the churches in New England, 1745;" "Vindication of divers Important Doctrines," 1752; "The True Scripture Doctrine of Original Sin, in answer to Dr. John Taylor, 1757." He was grandfather of Rev. Samuel Niles, of Abington, who died Jan. 16, 1814, aged 70, and of Judge Nathaniel Niles of Fairlee, Vt., who died Oct. 31, 1828, aged 88. The first President Adams, who personally knew him, observed of him, "I then revered and still revere the honest, virtuous and pious man." Rev. John Barnard, of Mar-

The following is a list of members in full communion with the Church at the time of Mr. Niles' settlement:

MALES.

Caleb Hubbard, Dea.,
Joseph Allen, Dea.,
Samuel Bass,
Nehemiah Hayden,
Edmund Littlefield,
Thomas Nash,
Samuel Allen,
Ephraim Thayer,
Peter Hubbard,
Samuel Niles,

Samuel Paine,
Theophilus Curtis,
Josiah Faxon,
William Thayer,
John Niles. 2d.,
Francis Nash,
John Hollis,
John Hayden,
Samuel Thompson,
Samuel French,

Thomas Wales,
John Thayer,
Ebenezer Spear,
John Niles,
Benjamin Niles,
William Nightingale,
Samuel Nash,
Thomas White,
Ebenezer Thayer.

FEMALES.

Mrs. —— Hubbard,
Lydia Allen,
Bethiah Bass,
Rebecca Nightingale,
Mrs. —— Spear,
Elizabeth French,
Widow —— Durin,
Mrs. Hollis,
Widow —— Thayer,

Hannah Hayden,
Hannah Curtis,
Mehitable Faxon,
Mary Niles,
Mary Jones,
Mary Nash,
Mrs —— Vining,
Mrs. —— White,
Sarah Thayer,

Mrs. —— Wales,
Sarah Towers,
Elizabeth Littlefield,
Mary Bagley,
Rachel Spear,
Susannah Nash,
Sarah Wild,
Abigail Allen,
Abigail Bass.

At what period the half-way covenant was adopted by the Church, does not appear from the records. It was in use, however, during the whole of Mr. Niles' ministry, and was not given up till several years after his death. It seems not to have been in a high degree popular, since the average number of admissions was but about six a year.

The following is the record, made by Mr. Niles, of admissions to full communion during his ministry:

1712.
Hannah Spear.

1713.
Wid. Margaret Thayer,
Mary Thayer.
Mary Wales,
Lydia Paine,
Mehitable Paine,
Samuel Wild,
George Chessman.

1714.
Jonathan Hayward,
Richard Thayer,
Hannah Faxon,
Thomas Vinton.

1715.
William Hunt,
Benjamin Allen,
Mrs. Jemima Clark,
Mrs. Jemima Clark, 2d.,

1715.
Elkanah Wales,
Elizabeth Wales,
Mrs. Sarah Ludden,
John Holbrook,
John Wild. Jr.,
Mrs. Sarah Hunt,

1716.
Rebecca Thayer,
Hannah Thayer,
Samuel White, Dea.

blehead, places him among the excellent ministers of New England; of whom he says, "these were all men of learning; pious, humble, prudent, faithful and useful men in their day." It may be added, that tradition reports him to have looked, · with distrust, on the "new measures" adopted by not a few men of eminent piety and zeal, during the period of "the great awakening," in the former part of the last century, and to have declined the opening of his pulpit to Whitefield and other shining lights of that day, lest the progress of truth and godliness among his people should be rather hindered than promoted. Probably this is true, as it well comports with the conservative character of a thoroughly read theologian and an acute metaphysician, who had already passed the grand climacteric of life. It should not be forgotten, however, that his error in judgment was followed by a fearful suspension of the special influences of the Holy Spirit as they appear in the glory of "the revival," for some sixty years.

1717.
None.

1718.
John Wild, Sen.,
Mary French.

1719.
Mrs. Mary Thayer,
Dependance French,
Mrs. Mary Thayer, 2d,
Mrs. Deborah Faxon,
Thomas Hunt,
Susannah Thayer,
Jonathan Bass,
Susannah Bass.

1720.
Thomas Wales,
Mrs. Mary Wales,
Mrs. Bethiah Wild,
Mrs. Jane Chessman,
Mrs. Sarah Newcomb,
Mrs. Abigail Penniman,
Phillip Thayer,
Mrs. Ruth Wild.

1721.
Mrs. Anna French,
Thomas Holbrook,
Mrs. Rachel Thayer,
Jonathan Wild,
Mrs. Sara Wild.
Mrs. Lydia Thayer,
Mrs. Sarah Hayden.

1722.
Josiah Hobart, Sen.

1723.
Elizabeth Linsfield.

1724.
Joseph White,
John Webb,
Mary Webb,
Joshua Hayward,
Mrs. Elizabeth Hayward,
Jonathan Clark,
Nathaniel Blanchard, Jr.,
Mrs. Sarah White,
Thomas French,
Mrs. Mary French.

1725.
Walter Mortamore.
Samuel Bass,
David Stone,
Mary Hayward,
Mrs. Mary Bowditch,
Mrs. Sarah Paine,
Shadrach Thayer,
Mrs. Rachel Thayer,
Lydia Thayer,
Richard Faxon.

1726.
Christopher Thayer,
Benjamin Hunt,
Mrs. Sarah Hunt.

1727.
Mary Powel,
Mrs. Sarah Arnold,
Mrs. Zipporah Curtis,
William Copeland,
Esther Thayer,

1728.
Hannah Houghton.
Mrs. Elizabeth Faxon,
Samuel Thayer.

1729.
Abigail Doggett,
Mrs. Elizabeth Thayer,
Benjamin Clark,
Mrs. Mary Clark,
Joseph Thayer,
John Trask,
Mrs. Penelope Trask,
Rebecca Spear.

1730.
Mrs. Mary French,
Atherton Wales,
John Hunt,
Mrs Rebecca Hunt,
Joseph White, Jr.,
Mrs. Hannah Bass,
Mary Thayer.

1731.
Mrs. Ruth Hunt,
John Thayer, Jr.,
Anna French,
Mrs. Rebecca French,
Mrs. Ruth Penniman,
Mrs. Elizabeth Hobart.

1732.
John Ludden,
Nathaniel Wales,
Samuel Wales.
Mrs. —— Wales,
Ebenezer Thayer,
James Bagley,
Mrs. Rachel Thayer,
Mary Jones,
Mrs. Sarah Hayden,
Mrs. Mary Jones,
Abigail White,
Mrs. Mary Hunt,
Peter Thayer,
Eunice Ludden.

1733.
Mrs. Anna Thayer,
Mrs. Priscilla Hayden,
Micah Allen,
Bathsheba Kilbee,
Mrs. Sarah Ludden,
Abigail Thayer,
Mrs. Ann Nash,
Seth Copeland,
Benjamin Copeland,
Benjamin Nash,
Ebenezer Hayden,
Mrs. Mary Hayden,
Elizabeth Green.

1734.
Ephraim Jones,
Isaiah Thayer,
James Thayer,
Abigail Clark,
James Penniman,
Thomas Allen,
Mrs. Hepzibah French,
Samuel White, Jr.

1735.
Widow Sarah Allen,
Samuel Curtis,
Mrs. Grace Curtis,
Mrs. Mary Thayer,
Mrs. Mary Allen.

1736.
William Allen,
John White,
Hannah Blanchard,
Mary Blanchard,
Judith Dorman,
John Holbrook Jr.

1737.
Joseph Hayward,
Samuel Hayden, Jr.,
Mrs. Mary Bowditch,
Ruth Whitmarsh.

1738.
James Thayer,
Moses French,
Edward Faxon,
Elisabeth Faxon,
Mrs. Abigail Thayer,
Mrs. Elizabeth Niles,
Nathan Whiting,
Mrs. Mary French,
John Blanchard,
Mary Blanchard,
Mrs. Susannah Copeland,
Nathaniel Thayer,
Mrs. Mary Thayer,
Mrs Sarah Copeland,
Mrs. Hannah Thayer,
Mrs. Sarah Hayward.

1739.
William Noyes,
William Bowditch,
Mary Dorman,
Mehitabel Vinton,
Jonathan Allen.

1740.
Penelope (colored woman),
John Capen,
Mrs. Ruth Capen.

1741.
Samuel Arnold,
Sarah Thayer,
Mrs. Bethiah Arnold,
Mrs. Christiana Thayer,
Ruth Capen,
Sarah Holbrook.

1742.
Ruth Wild,
Anna Wild,
John Noyes,
Elisha Niles,
Benjamin Thayer,
Sarah Capen,
Esther Capen,
Anna Thayer,
Ruth Thayer,
Elizabeth Bowditch,
Elizabeth Ludden,
Anna Ludden,
Mary Bowditch,
Abigail Owen,

1742.
Ruth Thayer,
Samuel Niles, Jr.
1743.
Hannah Thayer,
Mary Robinson,
Dr. Benjamin Ludden,
Ebenezer Whitmarsh,
Mrs. Hannah Niles,
John Hollis,
John Newcomb,
Mrs. Mary Newcomb,
Mary Whitmarsh,
Mrs. Ruth Clark.
1744
Mrs. Sarah Hunt,
Priscilla Faxon,
Ebenezer Newcomb,
Benjamin Clark, Jr.,
Mrs. Bethiah Clark.
1745
Samuel Wild, Jr.,
Mrs. Susanna Wild,
Deborah Ludden,
Mrs. Mary Holbrook.
1746.
Abigail Arnold,
Widow Abigail Thayer,
• Mrs Rachel Thayer,
Widow Sarah Trask,
Mrs. Rachel Hayden,
Ebenezer Thayer and
his wife.
1747.—None.

1748.
William White,
Mrs. Sarah White,
Thomas Thayer,
Mrs. Lydia Thayer,
Richard Faxon, Jr.,
Joanna Thayer,
Elizabeth Thayer,
Hannah Blanchard,
Abigail Blanchard,
Benj. Hayden and wife,
John Field and his wife.

1749.
Micah Thayer,
Mrs. Deborah Thayer,
Ephraim Hunt,
Mrs. Miriam Hunt,
Micah French.
1750.
Mrs. Rachel Sawin.
1751.
John Hayward,
Mrs. Elizabeth Thayer,
Mrs. Mary Allen,
Mrs Susannah White.
1752.
Mrs. Mary Spear,
Widow Hannah Hollis.
1753.
Nathaniel Wales,
Widow Hannah Stevens.
1754.—None.

1755.
Micah Wild,
Mrs. Rachel Wild,
Mrs. Joanna Ludden,
Mrs. Sarah Thayer.
1756
Hannah Hayward,
Rebecca Hunt,
Samuel Hunt,
Mrs. Hannah Hunt,
Benjamin Allen,
Mrs. Deborah Allen,
Benjamin Ludden,
Mrs. Deborah Wild,
Mrs Zilpah Thayer,
Ann Capen,
Thomas Vinton, Jr.,
Johnathan Thayer,
Enoch Hayden,
Mrs Amey Hayden.
1757.
David Holbrook, Jr.,
Widow Jane Noyes,
Sarah Thayer,
Richard Thayer, Jr.,
Mrs. Esther Thayer,

1757.
Samuel Hunt,
Caleb Thayer,
Mrs. Abigail Thayer,
George Hunt,
Elisha French,
Mrs. Mary French,
Mrs. Elizabeth Hollis
Mrs. Mary Denton,
Joseph Ludden, Jr.,
Atherton Thayer,
Mrs. Ruth Thayer,
Moses French, Jr.,
Mrs. Elizabeth French,
Mrs. Sarah Thayer,
Anna Wales.

1758.
Silas Wild,
Mrs. Ruth Wild,
Mrs. Dorcas Thayer,
Mrs. Deborah Wild,
Mrs. Lydia Pratt,
Ichabod Holbrook,
Mrs. Hannah Holbrook,
Mrs. Rachel Hollis,
Randal Wild.

1759.
Ephraim Blanchard.

1760.
Anna French.

1761.
Hobart Clark,
Richard Faxon, Jr.,
Jesse Wild,
Mrs. Judith Wild,
Wid. Margaret Thompson,
Nathaniel Capen,
Mrs. Deborah Capen,
Sarah Thayer.

1762.
Mrs. Esther Thayer,
Mrs. Sarah Penniman.

OFFICERS OF THE CHURCH DURING REV. MR. NILES' MINISTRY.

Peter Hobart and Samuel White were chosen deacons April 28, 1719.

William Hunt and John Holbrook were chosen deacons October 13, 1742.

James Penniman and Jonathan Allen were chosen deacons July 14, 1757; and on the 16th of the same month Thomas Allen was chosen to the same office, in conjunction with them.

John Holbrook, Jr., was chosen to the same office February 8, 1761.

Beside these officers, whose time of election is recorded, there were others who held the same office—how many, and what were their names, cannot now be ascertained. Incidental notices only, apprise us of the *fact* that the records are defective in this point.

Joseph Allen was the first deacon of the Church ; and died March 22, 1726, in the 77th year of his age. Mr. Niles subjoins, " He with others, made up the first hundred."

Elkanah Wales was also a deacon, but at what period is not known. He was once suspended from his office, and afterwards restored.

Jonathan Hayward was also a deacon ; and died July 13, 1757, in the 90th year of his age.

From September 3, 1758, to July 1, 1759, the administration of the Lord's Supper was suspended, owing to the pulling down of the old Meeting-house, and setting up a new one ; which was first used Thursday, June 28, 1759.

The Rev. Mr. Niles administered the ordinance of the Supper 301 times, during his ministry ; baptized about 1200 persons ; and received 312 to full communion.

Mr. Ezra Weld succeeded Rev. Mr. Niles, and was inducted into the pastoral charge Nov. 17, 1762. He was a native of Pomfret, Conn ; born June 13, 1736 ; and graduated at Yale College, in 1759.

The unanimity of the call is certified by the parish-book— in the absence of any church record on the subject—in words following :

" Aug. 19, 1762. Voted, by written votes, for a minister in this place ; and every vote was for Mr. Ezra Weld : which vote concurred with the Church's vote, Aug. 11, 1672, and consisted of fifty members, forty-seven of which voted for Mr. Weld ; the others did not act, being of the opinion we were too hasty in our proceedings."

Eleven Churches were requested to assist in the ordination ; viz., three in *Pomfret Con. ;* the Church in *Danvers,* Rev. Mr. Clark ; *Canton,* Rev. Mr. Dunbar ; *Weymouth,* Rev. Mr. Smith ; *Bridgewater,* Rev. Mr. Porter ; *Abington,* Rev. Mr. Dodge ; *Milton,* Rev. Mr. Robbins ; *Quincy,* Rev. Mr. Wibird ; *Randolph,* Rev. Mr. Taft.

The ordination sermon was delivered by Rev. Josiah Whitney, of Pomfret, from 2 Timothy, ii. 3. " Endure hardship as a good soldier of Jesus Christ."

During the early part of Mr. Weld's Ministry, the half-way covenant scheme—that most happy device for filling up the Church with hypocrites, and the world with infidels—was steadily and firmly assailed, till, in 1768, May 18th, the Church came to the following vote, viz. :

" The Church will receive those only to own the covenant, who are in a judgment of charity partakers of such qualifica-cations as entitle them to the benefits of all the ordinances, however they themselves may not see their way clear to come to the Lord's Supper; and that, in such cases, it is expected by the Church that they be in the use of all appointed means for the clearing of their scruples respecting that; and, by their endeavoring the same, the Church promise to exercise a tender and affectionate forbearance towards them in that respect."   *Attest*,   E. WELD, *Clerk.*

Subsequent to the passing of this vote, it is understood that none came into the Church, except through the "strait gate."

1795, *Sept.* 6. The Church appointed a Standing Committee, " to be assisting in any difficulties, which, in future, may arise between the members of the Church." The brethren chosen for this Committee were five, viz.: Deacons Moses French. Caleb Hayward, and Adam Hobart, and brethren Silas Wild, and Elisha French.

PROCEEDINGS OF THE CHURCH IN REFERENCE TO THE CALL OF REV. S. SAGE.

Sept. 2, 1807. A meeting of the Church was held this day, being opened with prayer for light and direction in the choice of a colleague pastor, by the moderator. The following votes were then passed, viz. :

1. To desire the Rev. Sylvester Sage, who has been preaching to us sometime, to settle with us in the work of the Gospel ministry.

2

2. That Gen. Ebenezer Thayer, David P. Hayward, Elisha French, Dea. Adam Hobart and Lemuel Veazie, brethren, be a committee to report to Rev. Mr. Sage the doings of the Church, and agree with him upon the conditions on which he will settle with us; and, also, make request to the town, at their meeting, Monday next, [to unite in the call].

Attest,   E. WELD, *Pastor.*

Sept. 25. The Church met, and voted that the Installation be [held] on the first Wednesday in November next. 2d, that the following Pastors and Churches be sent to : Rev. Dr. Porter, *Roxbury ;* Rev. Mr. Reynolds, *Wilmington ;* Rev. Mr. May, *Marblehead ;* Rev. Mr. Emerson, *Reading ;* Rev. Mr. Niles, *Abington ;* Rev. Mr. Norton, *N. Weymouth ;* Rev. Mr. Williams, *S. Weymouth ;* Rev. Mr. Strong, *Randolph ;* Rev. Mr. Whitney, *Quincy.* These, and a few others, viz.: Rev. Mr. French, of Andover; Rev. Mr. Emerson, of Boston; Rev. Mr. Peirce, of Brookline ; Rev. Dr. Thayer, of Kingston, N. H. ; and Rev. Mr. Gile, of Milton (afterwards invited), constituted the Council. Rev. Mr. Niles was chosen Moderator, and Rev Mr. Norton, Scribe.

The doings of the Church and town in the case were read ; the dismission and recommendation of Rev. Mr. S., given by the Church in Westminster, Vermont, were presented, together with his confession of faith. He was then examined more particularly as to his religious sentiments, and experimental religion.

It was then voted, " That the Council were ready to proceed to the services of the installation."

The introductory prayer was assigned to the Rev. Mr. French ; the sermon to Rev. Mr. May ; the charge to Rev. Mr. Williams; the consecrating prayer to Rev. Dr. Thayer ; the right hand of fellowship to Rev. Mr. Strong ; the concluding prayer to Rev. Mr. Whitney.

The pastoral relation of Mr. Sage to this Church was brief, continuing but eighteen months, and terminating May 4, 1809. This was owing to no fickleness of purpose on his part, nor to dissatisfaction or alienation on the part of the people, but entirely to failure of health in his family, consequent upon the change of a dry, inland climate, for the more damp and heavy atmosphere of the sea-coast.

The Council called for his dismission, of which Rev. Mr. Williams was Moderator, and Rev. Mr. Strong, Scribe, say, in their result:

" Under existing circumstances, Rev. S. Sage is called in duty to request that the ministerial relation between himself and the Church and Congregation in Braintree should be dissolved, and that the society stand justified in granting his request."

The Council add: " We rejoice that no impeachment is attached, either to the moral or ministerial character of Mr. Sage ; and most heartily recommend him to any people where he may be called to labor, as a wise, prudent, and faithful minister of the Gospel."

" We are happy to add, that the conduct of the Church and town of Braintree, under the trying dispensation of divine Providence which renders the dismission of their pastor necessary, has in our opinion been such as to reflect honor on themselves, and to meet our entire approbation."

Four persons were admitted to the Church, during his ministry. viz. :

1808.	1809.
Mr. Caleb Thayer,	Mr. Obadiah Thayer,
Mrs. Anna Holbrook.	Mrs. Betsy Thayer.

The baptisms, during the same term, were 27.

It is worthy of record, that the Rev. Mr. Sage was born in Berlin, Con., in 1766 ; graduated at Yale College, in 1787 ; was settled over the Congregational Church, in Westminster (East,) Vt., Oct. 13, 1790 ; and, with the exception of the time spent in Braintree, was sole clergyman of that parish, till near his death. October 13, 1800, he preached his semi-centennial sermon, and died January 21, 1841. Not only was he steadfast in his adherence to the faith once delivered to the saints—faithful in delivering the whole counsel of God, and earnest in enforcing the claims of the Gospel on the heart and conscience ; but in spirit he was kind and affectionate, in manners dignified and courteous, and in his wide-spread intercourse with the high and the low, the rich and the poor, he commanded universal respect and confidence : while among the intimates of his life, he was the object of most ardent affection,

At the time of Mr. Sage's induction to the pastoral office here, no record could be found, if any had been kept, of those who had been admitted to the watch and fellowship of the Church. By much and laborious inquiry, Mr. S. obtained some seventy names, of those who claimed, and were allowed, a place among the professed disciples of Christ.

INTERIM.

After the dismission of Mr. Sage, numerous candidates were employed for short terms.

While the Church were destitute of an active pastor, they passed the following vote, Feb. 5, 1810, viz. :

" No person. being a member of any other Church, shall commune with this Church at the Lord's table more than once after the passing of this vote, without a certificate from the Church to which he belongs."

At the same meeting, the Church solemnly renewed its covenant ; and being aware of the dangers that threatened the Churches, from errors newly brought in, and deceitfully propagated, by men who called themselves still ministers of Jesus Christ, the following articles of faith were agreed upon, and subscribed to, by the Church : —

CHURCH CONFESSION.

ARTICLE I. We believe in the existence of but one God, the Creator, Upholder, and Governor of all worlds and beings ; and that he is unchangeably possessed in the highest degree of all perfections, natural and moral.

Deut., vi. 4 ; Isa., xliii. 8 ; Heb., iii. 4, i. 3 ; Mal., iii. 6 ; John, iii. 27 ; Rev., iv. 8.

ART. II. We believe that there is a Trinity of persons, the Father, Son, and Holy Ghost, whose mysterious union is such as to constitute them but one God.

Matt., xxviii. 19 ; 3 Cor , xiii. 14 ; Matt., vii. 21, viii. 29, xiv. 33 ; John, i. 1—3 ; Isa., ix. 6 ; Acts, v. 31 , 2 Cor., iii. 17.

ART. III. We believe that the books contained in the Bible (which is in common use) were all given by inspiration of God, and that they contain a complete and consistent system of truths for the regulation of our faith and practice.

Tim., iii. 16 ; John, v. 39, xvii. 17 ; Rev., xvii. 18. 19.

ART. IV. We believe, that known unto God were all his
works from the beginning; that he made all things for himself; that he governs all things according to the counsel of his
own will, and therefore that we have the highest reasons for
the exercise of holy joy and rejoicing.

Isa., xliii. 6, 7; Rom., xi. 36; Acts, xv. 18; Dan., iv. 35; Psalms, xxxiii. 11;
Rev., xix. 1, 2.

ART. V. We believe, that God created our first parents in
his own image, perfectly upright in a moral view ; and that
by transgressing his righteous command, they lost that image,
became sinful, and justly exposed themselves to his everlasting wrath and curse.

Gen., i. 26, 27, 31 ; Eccl., vii. 29; Col., iii. 10; Gen., 2, 17, iii. 3, 6.

ART. VI. We believe that, in consequence of the first
transgression, all mankind in their natural state are the subjects of that carnal mind, which is enmity against God, not
subject to his law, neither indeed can be, and therefore that
by nature they are the children of wrath.

Rom., v. 12, 15—18; Gen., vi. 5, 11—13, and viii. 21; Matt., viii. 22; Tit., 1, 16;
John, iii. 6, 19; Col., 2, 13.

ART. VII. We believe, that all who are saved from wrath,
and obtain everlasting life, are those saved by the sovereign
mercy of God, through the atonement which was effected by
the obedience, sufferings and death of Christ.

Matt., xxvi. 28; Rom. vii. 32, iii. 24; Eph., i. 7, ii. 5, 8; Peter, i. 13, 19; Acts,
xx. 28; John, i. 16; Titus, iii. 7; 1 Peter, v. 10, 12.

ART. VIII. We believe, that notwithstanding the pro-
visions of the Gospel are sufficiently ample for the salvation
of sinners of every description, yet that none will accept the
salvation thus provided, but those only who are made willing
by the special and renewing influences of the Holy Spirit.

Rev., xxii. 17; Isa., xlv. 22; John, iii. 19, v. 40, vi. 44, x. 3; Gal., vi. 15; Titus,
iii. 5: 2 Peter, i. 10.

ART. IX. We believe, that those only will accept the
great salvation by truly believing in Jesus Christ, who are
ordained to eternal life ; and that all such believers will be
kept by the power of God unto salvation.

Acts, xiii. 48; Eph., i. 4, 5, 11; Matt., xx. 23; Rom., viii. 1; John, iv. 14, vi. 37
1 Peter, i. 5; Heb., x. 39; Col. iii. 3.

ART. X. We believe, that none ought to be admitted to a
visible standing in the Church of Christ, but such as in the

judgment of Christian charity are the subjects of faith, or a moral change of heart; and that none but those who are admitted to such a standing, have a right to the Lord's Supper, and baptism for their children.

Matt., xvi. 18: Acts, ii. 47; 1 Cor., i. 2; Gen., xxii. 10; Rom., iv. 11, xi. 17—42; 1 Peter, iii. 21; Heb. ix. 10.

ART. XI. We believe, that in God's own appointed time there will be a general resurrection of the bodies, both of the righteous and the wicked; that they will stand before the judgment seat of Christ; that they will by him be impartially judged, and sentenced to a just and final retribution, according to the respective deeds they had done in the Body; and that the wicked will go away into everlasting, or endless punisnment, but the righteous into life eternal.

Isa., xxvi. 19; Matt., xxii. 29—33; Rev., xx. 12; Eccl., ix. 9, xii. 14; Acts, xvii. 31; Matt., xxv. 31—16; Dan., xii. 2, 3; Rev., xx. 4, xxii 11.

ART. XII. Believing, as we do, that the above articles comprise the fundamental doctrines of the Bible, we give our solemn assent and consent to them.

We also solemnly pledge ourselves to each other, that we will not invite any man to take the oversight of us, or to be our pastor, whose religious sentiments, in our opinion, essentially differ from those above specified, and unto which we subscribe our respective names.

COVENANT.

Under the influence, we trust, of the truths contained in the preceding articles; with a view to our own edification and growth in grace; with a view to honor Christ, to advance his kingdom, and to glorify God,

We do now solemnly devote ourselves to the great Jehovah in the Covenant of Grace; we do cordially embrace the Lord Jesus Christ as our Redeemer, and final Judge; and the Holy Ghost as our Sanctifier, Comforter, and Guide.

We do religiously and solemnly promise, that by Divine assistance, we will renounce all fellowship with the unfruitful works of darkness, and walk as children of the light, and adorn the doctrine of God our Savior in all things, all the days of our lives, that others seeing our good works, may glorify our Father, who is in heaven.

We do also solemnly engage to maintain mutual watchfulness over each other,—in the spirit of brotherly love and Christian charity; and that in maintaining Christ's discipline, we will adopt, execute and submit to, that mode which is pointed out in the eighteenth chapter of Matthew, which we consider as eminently calculated to promote the best interests of his Church.

Thus we solemnly covenant, humbly imploring the Great Head of the Church, that he would impart to us wisdom and grace, faithfully to perform the vows which are upon us.

Ezra Weld, Pastor,	Robert Hayden,	David P. Hayward,
Isaac Thayer,	Jesse Pratt,	Adam Hobart,
Lemuel Veazie,	Solomon Thayer,	Levi Wild,
Jonathan Wild,	Caleb Thayer,	Eliphaz Thayer,
Samuel Pratt,	Obadiah Thayer,	Richard Thayer,
Elisha French,	Elisha French, jr.,	Asa French.
Daniel Fogg,		

The following form of covenant, differing slightly from the above, has been invariably read and accepted, on occasion of the admission of new members, since July, 1811, with the full consent and approbation of the Church :

COVENANT.

You do now, in presence of the heart-searching God, and before angels and men, choose the Lord Jehovah to be your God and portion; and you do hereby receive the Lord Jesus Christ for your Redeemer and Savior, and the Holy Spirit for your Teacher and Sanctifier.

You do wholly and openly renounce the power of sin and Satan, and resolve to live in universal obedience to all the Divine commandments.

You do submit to the government of Christ in his Church, and to the regular administration of it, at all times.

You covenant to attend the worship and ordinances of the Gospel with the Church, so long as God continues you in the world, and you are able to do it.

You promise to be accountable to this Church of Christ so long as you live, unless regularly dismissed from it.

Thus you covenant and promise, before God and his people

[Here the brethren and sisters of the church rise in their places, in token of their cordial admission of the candidate to their privileges; and the pastor adds :]

In behalf then of this Church. and by the authority of Him who sitteth on the holy hill of Zion, I say to you—

We do now receive you affectionately into our communion and fellowship; and we promise to watch over you with all Christian tenderness, treating you as a member of the body of Christ, according to his commandment; and expecting from you a cheerful reciprocation of all the kind offices required by the fraternal relation into which a gracious God permits us to enter.

"The Lord bless thee, and keep thee; the Lord make his face to shine upon thee, and be gracious unto thee; the Lord lift up his countenance upon thee, and give thee peace!"

[If the occasion require, or the impulses of the heart prompt further utterances of brief counsel or exhortation, the pastor is at liberty to "speak on."]

1810. *May* 22. At a meeting of the Church, fifteen members being present, it was voted "to give Mr. Allen [then holding office in Harvard university] a call to settle with us in the Gospel ministry; eleven members voting for it." This call was declined; and soon after, Mr. Allen was chosen to the Presidency of Dartmouth College, and after a few years service, was elected to the same office in Bowdoin College, at Brunswick, Me., where he accomplished much for God and his generation. He still lives, and though not occupying a public station, devotes himself to literary and religious labors for the benefit of present and future generations.

Oct. 18. "The Church met, and voted unanimously to give Mr. R. S. Storrs a call to settle with them in the Gospel ministry." The town was requested to unite with them in said call.

The call was accepted—on condition that the pastor elect be at liberty to fulfill an engagement he had made, for six months' missionary service, in the State of Georgia. This condition was accepted by the Church.

Mr. Gordon Hall, who at this time was waiting a fit opportunity to proceed on his mission to India, consented to supply the pulpit during its six months' vacancy; and never was it more usefully or acceptably filled. His name will be had in everlasting remembrance.

1811. *April* 26. The Church met, and voted " to set apart the first Wednesday in June, for the ordination of Mr. Storrs , " ° also, " to send letters for assistance in the ordination," to certain pastors and Churches.

The " letters missive " were responded to by the following pastors and their Churches, viz.: Rev. Mr. Niles, *Abington ;* Rev. Mr. Williams, *Weymouth ;* Rev. Mr. Norton, *N. Weymouth ;* Rev. Mr. Strong, *Randolph ;* Rev. Mr. Codman, *Dorchester ;* Rev. Mr. Gile, *Milton ;* Rev. Mr. Storrs, *Longmeadow ;* Rev. Mr. Reynolds, *Wilmington ;* and Rev. Dr. Griffin, *Boston.*

Rev. Mr. Williams was chosen Moderator, and Rev. Mr. Norton, Scribe, with Rev. Mr. Codman, assistant scribe.

After the usual devotional exercises, the proceeedings of the Church and parish in relation to the call were read, and a verbal declaration of acceptance was made by Mr. Storrs before the Council: who also presented a written confession of his faith. " The Council, having attended to these things, and having obtained satisfaction, that Mr. Storrs is a regular member of the Church of Christ, and that he has been licensed by the Presbytery of Long Island to preach the Gospel, voted to proceed to ordination."

The introductory prayer was offered by Rev. Mr. Strong ; the sermon was delivered by Rev. R. S. Storrs, sen. ; the consecrating prayer was offered by Rev. Mr. Niles; the charge to the pastor, by Rev. Mr. Williams ; fellowship of the Churches, by Rev. Mr. Norton ; concluding prayer, by Rev. Mr. Gile. The irrelevant service of " a charge," or " address to the people," in those days was an unknown work of superrogation.

The object of this " manual " being the preservation of *facts,* it may not be out of order to note the following, though of little importance.

Mr. Storrs was born in Longmeadow, Feb. 6, 1787 ; graduated at Williams College, 1807 ; first studied theology with Rev. Dr. Woolworth, of Bridgehampton, L. I. ; was licensed by the Suffolk Presbytery; supplied the then collegiate pulpits of Smithtown and Islip six months ; afterwards spent a year and an half in the Theological Seminary at Andover, leaving that Institution in Sept., 1810.

° At the request of the pastor elect, this day was changed to Wednesday, July 3d.

LIST OF CHURCH MEMBERS.

ABBREVIATIONS, dec. deceased,—dis. dismissed,—ex. excluded,—L, Letter.

Rev. Ezra Weld,	dec.	1816
Elisha, s. of M. French,	"	1818
Richard, s. of R. Thayer,	"	1823
David P., s. of J. Hayward,	dis.	1811
Robert, s. of B. Hayden,	dec.	1822
Gaius, s. of T. Thayer,	ex.	1820
Ebenezer, s. of S. Thayer,	dec.	1809
Jesse, s. of J. Pratt,	"	1813
Lemuel, s. of B. Veazie,	"	1825
Dea. Adam, s. of C. Hobart,	"	1824
Dea. Eliphaz, s. of J. Thayer,	dis.	1811
Jonathan, s. of S. Wild,	dec.	1840
Isaac, s. of A. Thayer,	"	1827
Solomon, s. of J. Thayer,	"	1835
Levi, s. of R. Wild,	"	1848
Elisha, s. of E. French,	"	1826
Asa, s. of M. French,	"	1853
Samuel, s. of J. Pratt,	dis.	1815
Daniel, s. of J. Fogg,	dec.	1830
Caleb, s. of I. Thayer,	"	1852
Obadiah, s. of R. Thayer,	"	1841
Rachel, w. of E. Thayer,	"	1819
Elisabeth, w. of R. Hayden,	"	1820
Jemima, w. of T. Vinton,	"	1816
Mary, w. of N. Wales,	"	1841
Sarah, w. of L. Veazle,	"	1824
Phebe, w. of L. Veazie, Jr.,	"	1847
Miriam, w. of B. Hayden,	"	
Mehitabel, w. of D. Holbrook,	dis.	1811
Miriam, w. of C. Nash,	dec.	1819
Mehitabel w. of A. French,	"	1819
Lois, w. of D. P. Hayward,	dis.	1811
Elisabeth, w of N. Hayward,	dec.	1848
Abigail, w. of W. Allen,	dis.	1815
Mary, w. of D. Hayward,	dec.	1810
Eunice, w. of M. French,	"	1834
Rhoda, w. of L. Wild,	"	1840
Joanna, w. of J. Pratt,	dis	1815
Persis, w. of S. Pratt,	"	1815
Susannah, w. of E. French,	dec.	1818
Sarah, w. of E. Denton,	"	1831
Hannah, w. of A. Stetson,	dis.	1811
Rebecca, w of J. Bowditch,	"	1811
Relief, w. of S. Penniman,		
Elisabeth, d. of S. French,	dec.	1822
Dorcas, of Thayer,	"	1815
Deborah, w. of S. Wild,	"	1813
Rachel, w. of P. Wild,	"	1829
Ruth, w. of E. Penniman,	"	1839
Rachel, w. of A. Faxon,	"	1830
Deborah, w. of J. Wild,	"	1855
Deliverance, w. of Dea. E. Thayer,	dis.	1811
Lydia, w. of E. Harmon,	dec.	1829
Abigail, of Thayer,	"	1811
Mary, of Wild,	"	1828
Elisabeth, w. of T. Curtis,	"	1825
Sarah, w. of J. Hayward,	"	1812
Sarah, w. of T. Capron,	"	1830
Lucy, w. of S. Chessman,	"	1821

Anna, W. of E. Holbrook,	dec	
Alethea, of Hollis,	"	1816
Mary, of Holbrook,		
Hepzibah, w. of J. Vinton,	"	1808
Ruth, w. of J. Arnold,	"	1850
Sally, d. of J. Bowditch,	"	1848
Molly, d. of J. Pratt,	dis.	1815
Betsy, w. of O. Thayer,	dec.	1823
Susanna Fogg,	"	1856
Hannah Clark,	"	1842

1811

Rev. R. S., s. of Rev. R. S. Storrs,		
Ruth, w. of J. Denton,	dec.	1836
Ruth, d. of J. Hayward,	"	1818
Nathaniel E., s. of Richard Thayer,	"	1842
Avis, w. of Dea. A. Hobart,	"	1830
Betsy, w. of S. Thayer,		1847
Abigail, w. of V. J. Hollis,	dis.	

1812.

Dorcas, d. of N. Hayden,	"	
Benjamin, s. of N. Wales,	dec.	1833
Theodora, w. of B. Wales,	"	1848
Abraham, s. of A. Hobart,		
Sarah, w. of A. Hobart,	"	1821
Elisha, s. of A. Hobart,	dis.	1859
Ruth w. of E. Hobart,	dec.	1859
Thomas, s. of Hancock,	dis.	1855
Levi, s. L. Thayer,	"	1829
Relief, w. of J. Adams,	"	
Deliverance, w. of N. E. Thayer,		
Lucy, w. of French,		
Mary, d. of S. Chessman,		
Elisabeth, d. of B. French,	dec.	1825
Rachel, w. of S. Hayden,		
Betsy, w. of H. Hook r.	dis.	1820
Clarissa, w. of C. Hayward,		
Sally, w. of N. Wales, Jr.		
Barzillai, s. of W. Penniman,	dec.	1854
Mary, w. of B. Penniman,	"	1831
Elisha, s. of Z. Thayer,	"	1857
Susanna, w. of E. Thayer,	"	1857
David, s. of T. Hollis,	"	1858
Mary, w. of D. Hollis,	"	1847
Nehemiah, s. of N. Hayden,	"	
William, s. of B. Thayer,	dis.	1830
Ebenezer, s. of E. Denton,		
Sarah, w. of Arnold,	dec.	
Susanna, of Holbrook,		
Ruth, w. of E. Penniman,	"	1839
Suky, w. of S. French,	"	1829
Judith, w. of A. French,	"	1814
Sally, w. of E. Thayer,		
Lydia, w. of B. Bowditch,	dis.	
Elisabeth, D. of G. Thayer,	dec.	
Elisabeth, w of Smith,	dis.	
Elisabeth A., w. of N. Penniman,		
Margery, w. of C. White,	dec.	1840
Miriam, d. of B. Hayden,	"	1829

Phebe, w. of J. Sorter,
Abigail, w. of O. Hayden,
Suky, w. of C. Hollis,
Elisabeth, d. of E. Clark,   dec 1821
Rachel, w. of S. French,
Sarepta, w. of J. P. Newcomb,
Charlotte, of   Thayer,   dis
Sally, w. of R. Packard,   " 1829
Lydia, w. of P. Hollis,   dec 1829
Mehitabel, w. of J. Hobart,   " 1816
Huldah, w. of P. Hayden,   " 1851
Mary, w. of J. Dyer,   dis 1829
Mehitabel. of   Hayden,   " 1829
Lydia, w. of J. French,   dec 1850

1813.
Sarah S., w. of Rev. R. S.
   Storrs,   " 1818
Phebe, w. of J. Glover,   " 1852

1814.
Polly, w. of R. Arnold,   " 1857
Mary, w. of N. White,
Sally, w. of J. Dyer,   dis 1829

1815.
Mary, w. of R. Sugden,   "

1816.
Robert, s. of R. Hayden,   dec 1853
Nathaniel, s. of N. Thayer,   " 1817
Alice, w. of S. Capen,   " 1840
Elisabeth, w of   Stowel,   dis
Julia A., w. of Rev. T. De Witt,   "
Sally, w. of J. Hollis,
Atherton, s. of P. Wild,   " 1829
Lucy, w. of A. Wild,   " 1829
Harvey, s. of E. French,   dec 1824
Roland, s. of G. Packard,   dis
Eunice, w. of S. French,
Prudence, w. of M. Hunt,
Lydia, w. of J. Holbrook,   " 1850
Rachel, d. of E. Soper,   dec 1859
Rachel, w. of N. Hurd,   dis
Alethea W., d. of E Penniman,   dec 1819
Esther A. w. of E. Porter,
Deborah, d. of G. Thayer,   "
Rachel, d. of J. Sampson,   " 1856

1817.
Abigail F., w. of P. Davis,   dis
Livia D., d. of N. Thayer,
Ruth W., w. of N. Baxter,   dec
Rebecca, w. of S. V. Arnold.

1818.
Eliza, d. of A. French,   " 1820
Ebenezer T., s. of D. Fogg,   ex
Susan N., w. of E N. Thayer,
Mary, d. of J. Bowditch.

1819.
Esther, d. of D. Loring.

1820.
Alice, w. of J. Spear,   dec 1824
Rhoda, of   Holbrook,
Betsy, w. of J. Warren,   dis 1831
Harriet, w. of Rev. R. S.
   Storrs, D. D.   dec 1838

1821.
None.

1822.
Sarah, w. of O. Harding,
Sally, d. of E. Clark,   dec 1856
Elisabeth, of   Holbrook.
Huldah, w. of Z. Wild,   " 1832

1823.
Eunice, d. of N. Hayward.   " 1832

1824.
Silence, w. of S. Hayden,
Susan, w. of J. Hobart,   " 1842
Deborah, w. of S. Wild,   dis 1829
Dea. Charles, s. E. Dickerman, dec 1854

1825.
Esther, w. of J. Hayward,   dis 1830
Rebecca N., w. of Rev. J.
   Farnsworth,   "

1826.
Ruth, w. of J. Dyer,   " 1829
Hannah, d. of S. Thayer,

1827.
None.

1828.
Harlow, s. of   Hooker,   " 1829
Thomas s. of S. Penniman,   "
John, s. of C. Thayer.
Charles M., s. of D. Fogg,   dec. 1854
Ann, d. of J. Wild,   dis. 1829
Sally, w. of C. French,
Samuel, s. of R. Hayden,   dec 1859
Julia A., d. of S. Hayden,
Sarah, d. of   Fogg,   dis
Jerusha, w. of C. Paine,   dis 1830
Phebe N., D of J. Glover,   dec 1847
Esther, d. of Dea. N. E. Thayer,
Naomi, w. of E. Hobart,   dec 1859
Eliza, w. of E. Denton,   dis
Sylvia, w. of A Randal,   "
Asa, S. of A. Penniman,
Elisabeth H., w. of A. Penniman,   ex
Louisa, d. of S. Hayden,
Jerusha T., d. of N. Holbrook, dec 1844
Anthony, s. of A Dyke,   dis 1829
Mary, w. of A Dyke,   " 1829
Elisha, s. of S. Wild,   " 1829
Caroline, w. of E. Wild,   " 1829
Jonathan, s. of A. French,
Sarah B. w of J. French,
Nathaniel, s. of N. Hayward.
Abigail, w. of T Hancock,   dec 1833
Rachel, d. of L. Veazie,
Sarah J. d of S. Thayer,
Rebecca T. w. of C. Hayden,   dis.

1829.
Ebenezer, s. of J. Denton,   dis
Nancy A w of G. Thayer,
Susan H. w. of J. H J. Thayer, L
Mary, w. of G. Blanchard,   dec 1843
Mary, w of C. Faxon,   " 1847
Deborah, d. of L. Veazie.

1830.
Amos H. s. of C. Hunt,   L

1831.
Samuel, s. of A. Hayden,
Joseph H. J. s. of S. Thayer,   dis

Zimri, s. of A. Heath,   L
Ruth, w. of Z. Heath.   L
1832.
Samuel, s. of ——R. Hayden, dec 1859
Daniel H. s. of J. Denton,
Lemuel, s. of L. Veazie,
Dorcas, w. of N. Thayer,   dec 1840
Hannah d. of S Thayer,   dec 1850
Polly, w. of J. Denton,   dec 1850
Ruthy, w of E. Penniman,   dec 1839
Elizabeth, w. of A. H. Hunt,   dec 1842
Caleb, s. of T. Hollis,
George S. s. of N. Nason,   ex
Oliver, s. of O. Hayden,
Samuel, s. of S. French,
Emmons, s. of Dea. N. E. Thayer,
David, s. of Dea. N. E. Thayer,
Hiram, s. of Hunt,   ex
Thais. w. of J. Nottage,   dis
Rachel, w. of J. French,
Sarab, w. of ——Gooch,   dec 1841
Irene, w. of N. Bunker,
Beulah. w. of M. Arnold,
Deborah, w. of A. Hobart,
Mary, w, of J. Thayer,
Hannah, of Thayer,
Mary A., w. of O. Wilde,
Laura, d. of A. Penniman,   dec 1859
Beulah, d. of M. Arnold,
Harriet, d. of N. Wales,
Ann, d. of C. French,
Maria, d. of C. White,   ex
Ellen, d. of D. Gorham,
Sarah E d. of Dea. N. E. Thayer, dec 1841
Rhoda, d. of L. Veazie,
Deborah, d. of G. Thayer,
Lucinda, d. of E. F. Thayer,   dec 1845
Ruthy, d. of S. Snell,
William, s. of ——Nottage,   dec
Josiah, s. of ——Nottage,   dec
Asaph, s. of ——Goodenow,   dec 1854
Samuel D. s. of S. Hayden,
Ann, w. of S. D. Hayden,
Elisha, s. of E. French,
Lucinda, w. of E. French,
Josiah, s. of J. Hollis,
Elizabeth, w. of J. Hollis,
Margery A. d. of C. White,   dec 1857
Mary, w. of C. Dickerman,
Eunice, d. of J. Hollis,
Susan, d. of J. Hollis,
Susan, d. of E. Thayer,
Avis A. d. of E. Hobart,
Deborah. d. of Z. Wilde,   dec 1851
Mary A. w. of G. S. Nason,
Ellas, s. of N. Hayward,
Elizabeth D. w. of E. Hayward, dec 1859
Rev. Edwards A. s. of Rev. C. Park, D.D.
David. s. of ——Gorham,
Mrs. Hannah, w. of D. Gorham, dec 1835
1833.
None.
1834.
Elizabeth, d. of J. Bowditch,   dec 1847
Charlotte, w. of C. M. Fogg,

1834.
Richard, s. of J. Allen,
Elizabeth, w. of E. Lovell,   dec 1851
1835.
None.
1836.
Charles, s. of ——Dickson,   L
Rebecca. w. of C. Dickson,   L
Ann, w. of Rev. R. S. Storrs, D.D. L
Eliza, w. of B. F. Arnold,   dec L 1843
Rebecca, w. of S. Veazie,   dec L 1842
Sally, w. of N. Hayward,   L
1837.
Rowena, w. of B. Ryan,
Elizabeth, d. of N. Hayward,   dis
Nancy L. d. of J. Wild,   dec
1838.
Sarah H. d. of J. Thayer,
1839.
Jacob, s. of ——Abbott,   L dis
Harriet, w. of J. Abbott,   L dis
Hannah, w. of S. Barrel,   dis
Caroline, d. of J. Hollis.

1840.
Josiah, s. of R. Hayden,   L dec 1856
Dorcas, w. of J. Hayden,   L dec 1854
Hannah S. w. of J. Holbrook, L dec 1848
1841.
Charles A. s. of C. French,
Caroline, w. of B. V. French, L dec 1843
Sarah, d. of Dea. N. E. Thayer.
1842.
Jechonias, s. of S. Thayer,   L
Abby H. w. of J. Thayer,   dec L 1854
Eliza, d. of J. Thayer,   dec L 1847
Thomas A. s. of R. Hayden,   L
Mehitable, w. of T. A. Hayden,   L
Rebecca S. w. of C. Hayden,   L
Emily P. d. of S. Reynolds,   L dis
Dr. Jonathan, s. of J Wilde,
William, s. of ——Sawyer,
Lucy, w. of A. Penniman,   dec 1859
Mary, d. of J. Wilde,   dis
Nancy, d. of T. A. Hayden,
Sarah, w, of S. M. Capen,   dec
Elizabeth. d. of E. Penniman,
Rachel, d. of J. Bowditch,
Clarissa, d. of C. Hayward,
Merinda, d. of W. Holbrook,   ex
Enoch H s of E. Fisher,
Ann. w of E. H. Fisher.
Ebenezer F. E. s of E. F. E. Thayer,
Sarah S. S. w. of F. E. Thayer.
Sarah A. w. of D. H. Niles,
Nancy C. w. of T. Daniels,
Ruth, d. of E. Penniman,
Abigail, d. of C. Faxon,   dis 1850
Abby H. d. of J. Thayer,
Richard S., Jr., s. of Rev. R.S. Storrs, dis
Henry M. s. of Rev. C. B. Storrs, dis
Joseph C. s. of Rev. C Williams L
Sarah w. of J. C. Williams, L   dec 1856
Thomas, s. of J. Daniels,   L
Sarah B. C. w. of Rev. Thomas Noyes, L

1843.

Dea. Jonathan, s. of Jas. Cochran, L dis
Mary, w. Dea. J Cochrane, L dis
Lucy, w. of J. Hobart, L
1844.
Jane B., d. of C. French, L
Hannah, w. of J. Arnold, L
Mary H., d. S. White.
1845.
None.
1846.
None.
1847.
Louisa, w. of T. Martin, dis
1848.
Lucy, w. of Dea. D. Hollis.
1849.
Dr. Cyrus S., s. of Rev. C. Mann, L
Harriet F, w. of Dr. C. S. Mann, L
Frances B., w. of E Thayer, L
1850.
None.
1851.
Caroline, d. of C. Stetson.
Harriet, d. of J. Thayer.
Persis, d. of J. Thayer, dis
Eunice, d. of E. Hayward,
Dr. Alex. R., s. of Rev. S. Holmes, L
Ruth, d. of — Ricker,
Charles, s. of M. French, L
Catherine L., w. of C. French, L
Mary A., w. of W. Hollis, L
1852.
Caleb, s. of A. Stetson, L
Susan H., w. of C. Stetson, L
Sarah C. d. of C. French,
Sarah F., d. of E. Hayward, dis
Eunice C., d. of Rev. R. S. Storrs, L
Joseph A., s. of J. Hollis,
Sarah W., w of W. Gage,
Abigail L., d. of J. Wild.
1853.
Mary, d. of — Parsons, L
Fidelia, w. of A. H. Hunt, L
1854.
Edward, s. of C. Thayer,
William, s. of J. Kincald,
Laura A., w. of G. W. Currier, L

1855.

Maria, w. of P. Gilman,
Rhoda F., w. of H. Mann,
Lois, d. of C. Faxon,
Mary, w. of A. Arnold.

1856.
Frank W., s. of H. Reeves, L
Sarah E., w. of F Reeves, L
Norton, s of L. Pratt, L
Emeline M., w. of N. Pratt, L

1857.
Catherine V, w. of E. Potter,
Sophia, w. of T B. Vinton,
Sarah, w. of W. Kincald,
Sarah A.. d. of E C. Bowditch,
Caroline E., d. C. French,
Thomas B., s. of B. Vinton, L
Mercy L., w. of C. Briggs, L
Elvira, w. of E. Thayer, dec.
Charles W, s. of J. Hobart,
Adeline, d. of dea E. Hayward,
Hannah E., d. of S. Thayer.

1858.
Elisha A, s. of E. Belcher,
Mary F, w. of A. Belcher.
Susan A., w. J. E Holbrook,
Harriet M., w. of J Fogg,
Franklin E., s. of B. F Arnold,
Susannah N., d, of E. N. Thayer,
Sarah H, d. of E N. Thayer,
Mercy B, d. of O. Cobb,
Ann S, d. of dea E. Hayward,
Helen L., d. of C. Stetson,
Anna M, d. of C. Stetson,
Susan M., d. of R. Sherman,
Phebe A., d. of W. Sherman,
Sarah E., d. of J. Sampson, L

1859.
Henry M., s. of J. Hollis,
Eliza S., w. of A. Hobart,
Julia A., w. of S. Dustin,
Ruth, d. of N. Wales,
Della, w. of S. Thayer,
Harriet S., w. of —— Donnett,

ACTS OF THE CHURCH.

1814. *Sept.* 1. Brother David Hollis was chosen Deacon, in place of Deacon Hobart, who resigned an office he had long held and honorably fulfilled, on account of the increasing infirmities of age.

Same day. *Voted,* that the Deacons be required to keep regular accounts of the monies received at the sacramental collections, and that if there be an overplus, after defraying the

3

necessary expenses, it be subject to the disposal of the Church for the benefit of the poor.

1815. *Sept.* 1. Brother Nathaniel E. Thayer was chosen second Deacon, and set apart to the sacred office by prayer.

1817. *Sept.* 7. The Church *Voted*, To allow their Pastor to spend the third week in this month in Missionary labor, on the borders of Rhode Island.

1820. *May* 14. The Church *Voted*, To take the Sabbath School under their direction ; and appointed a Committee of five, to make and carry into effect arrangements for the present year.

1821. *July* 21. A Committee of seven was appointed, to report, next Lord's day, on the best method of securing a fair proportion of aid from this parish for the support of Mr. Temple, on his mission to Palestine. Deacons Hobart, Hollis, and Thayer, with brethren A. French, R. Hayden, Jr., L. Wild, and L. Thayer, were chosen.

1824. *Dec.* 2. The Church this day *Voted*, That a Committee of five be appointed, whose duty it shall be, in conjunction with the Pastor, to examine all persons offering themselves as candidates for admission to the privileges of the Church before they shall be propounded. ,

That it be the duty of this Committee to meet at least once in three months, and as much oftener as they may find it necessary or convenient.

That their meetings be open to any member of the Church who may wish to be present.

1827. *June* 3. The Church *Voted*, That they highly approve of the plan of Church Conference, which has been recently proposed by a Committee of the Norfolk Association.

Sept. 11. The Church Committee appointed a special meeting for baptised children, on the 22d inst., requesting also the attendance of their parents.

Though the proposed meeting was not numerously attended, owing to unfavorable weather, yet the attention and deep feeling manifested, evinced the presence of the Holy Spirit.

1828. *March* 5. This day was observed by the Church as a season of fasting, humiliation, and prayer, in reference to the state of religion among us. The morning was spent in fasting and prayer "by every one apart." At 11 o'clock, the Church met at the house of God, and spent two hours in prayer, confession, and renewal of covenant. At 2 o'clock, the congregation assembled, and a sermon was delivered by Rev. Mr. Green, of Boston. At half past 5 o'clock, the Church met again, and was addressed by several lay brethren from Boston. An evening service was also held, in which Rev. Mr. Green addressed the assembly; and many were constrained to say, "It is good to be here."

1829. *Jan.* 4. At a regular meeting of the Church, it was *Voted*, 1. That a quarterly collection be taken up in the congregation for the Massachusetts Missionary Society.

2. That a part of the proceeds of the Monthly Concert collections be appropriated to the same object.

May 4. At a regular church meeting, it was *Voted, unanimously*, That the Pastor be at liberty to be absent for six months during each of the two succeeding years, in aid of the cause of Home Missions, as an Agent of the American Home Missionary Society, it being understood that he furnish supplies for the pulpit.

1830. *Dec.* 29. The old meeting-house having been taken down by vote of the Parish, the new one, just completed, was this day solemnly dedicated to the service of Almighty God, Father, Son, and Holy Ghost. Introductory prayer by Rev. Mr. Perkins, of East Braintree; reading of the Scriptures by Rev. Mr. Huntington, of N. Bridgewater; dedicatory prayer by Rev. Dr. Codman, of Dorchester; sermon by the Pastor; concluding prayer by Rev. Mr. Matthews, of So. Braintree; the benediction by the Rev. Mr. Gile, of Milton. The day was pleasant and joyous. The sale of the pews exceeded the cost of the house, $1725.

1831. *Aug.* 4. On the question of the Pastor's dismission from the charge of this church, that he might accept the office of "Associate Secretary and General Agent of the American Home Missionary Society for the New England States"—it was voted, after much discussion, "That the church consent to the settlement of a colleague pastor, leaving the present pastor at liberty to devote himself to the duties of the proposed office for a term not exceeding five years — he relinquishing all pecuniary claims on the church and parish during that term. In this vote the parish concurred.

October 31. It was voted by the church unanimously, "That Mr. Edwards A. Park be invited to settle with us in the gospel ministry, as colleague pastor, on the conditions that he discharge all the duties of the pastoral and ministerial office, and relieve the senior pastor from all the responsibilities of said office, for a term not exceeding five years." This vote was concurred in by the parish unanimously.

This call was accepted by Mr. Park, with the following modification suggested by him and adopted by the other parties concerned, viz.: " That his connexion with the church and parish be not limited to five years, but continued so long as both parties agree to continue it, be the term more or less than five years."

December 21. This being the day appointed for the ordination of Mr. E. A. Park, the following churches were represented in council by pastors and delegates, viz.:

Bowdoin st. church—Rev. Dr. L. Beecher and delegate.
Park st. church, ——— ———, Josiah Hayden, del.
Dorchester—Rev. Dr. Codman, and del.
Milton—Rev. S. Gile, and del.
Dedham S.—Rev. H. G. Park, and del.
Stoughton—Rev. Dr. Park and del.
Easton—Rev. L. Sheldon, and del.
Randolph E.—Rev. D. Brigham, and del.
Randolph W.—Rev. Mr. Hitchcock, and del.
North Bridgewater—Rev. Mr. Huntington, and del.
Braintree S.—Rev. Mr. Matthews, and del.
Braintree and Weymouth, union—Rev. Mr. Perkins, and del.
Weymouth S.— ——— ———, a del.

The Council having been organized, by the choice of Dr. Park as Moderator, and L. Sheldon, Scribe, proceeded to the examination of the candidate; and, being satisfied therewith, assigned the several parts of the ordination service, as follows: to Rev. Mr. Perkins, the introductory prayer; to Rev. Dr Park, the sermon; to Rev. R. S. Storrs, the charge; to Rev. H. G. Park, the right hand of fellowship; to Rev. S. Gile, the consecrating prayer; and to Rev. Mr. Matthews, the concluding prayer.

On the part of the church, a day of fasting and prayer had been observed the week previous to the ordination, when they confessed their faults and sins one to another, and voted to hold a protracted meeting immediately after the ordination services were over; accordingly, meetings commenced on Wednesday evening, were continued to the close of the week, and happy results followed — even a general revival of religion.

1832. *January* 9. The church voted to instruct the standing committee to propound for admission to the church no one who would not pledge himself to a total abstinence from ardent spirits, except when used as a medicine.

December 28. The church appointed a committee of two, to "visit some communicants whose conduct deserved reprehension;" and voted to observe the seventh day of January ensuing as a day of fasting and prayer, for the revival of God's work.

1833. *December* 26. The junior pastor requested of the church a dismission from his charge; and the church voted to accede to his request, "tho' with feelings of painful regret."

1834. *January* 8. The parish having felt constrained, though reluctantly, to concur in the action of the church, Dec. 26, an ecclesiastical council was called, and met,

January 17—to consider the question of the junior pastor's dismission. Rev. Calvin Park, D. D., of Stoughton; Rev. Jonas Perkins, of Union church; Rev. L. Matthews, of So. Braintree; and Rev. John C. Phillips, of N. Weymouth, with the delegates of their churches, convened and organised, by choosing Rev. Dr. Park, Moderator, and the Rev. Mr. Phillips, Scribe. The request of Mr. Park, occasioned by an urgent invitation to a Professorship in Amherst College, and a conviction of his duty to accept it, was then laid before the council, together with the doings of the church and parish in the premises. The proceedings having been regular and satisfactory, the council voted the dissolution unanimously. Their result follows:

" Voted, That the council entertain a high sense of the faithfulness and devotedness of Rev. Mr. Park in the discharge of his pastoral duties—of his incessant and various labors to promote the intellectual and moral improvement of the people of his late charge, and they cordially recommend him to the fellowship and confidence of the churches of our Lord.   The council, in view of the connexion which has hitherto so happily subsisted between this church and the late junior pastor, and which has been so signally blessed by the God of all grace, cannot but sympathise with them in the dissolution of said connexion ; and knowing how happy this connexion has been to the present pastor, they would express their sympathy with him, in the loss which he has sustained, in the dismisson of so able and beloved a colleague.   And the council commend him, with his beloved church, to the guidance and care of Him who is able to sanctify to them this affliction, and to build them up in the faith and order of the gospel.

For about two years from the date of Rev. Mr. Park's dismission—and during the continued Home Mission Agency, and subsequent protracted illness of the pastor—the church and congregation were edified by the ministerial labors, chiefly, of the Rev. Paul Jewett and Mr. William R. Jewett, who successively "stood in the gap" and "fed the people with knowledge."   From that period the senior pastor resumed the duties of his office so far as reduced health would permit, relinquishing the Agency to which he stood pledged, after four years' exhausting service.

Few things deserving of special notice, in this connection, occurred, out of the ordinary routine of pastoral care.   Here and there cases of discipline arose, requiring firmness and forbearance on the part of the church ; and various action on incidental matters was taken from time to time, as the records will disclose to all whose curiosity or necessity may prompt to inquiry.

1841.   *December* 23.   The deacons of the church were appointed to act as a committee, in conjunction with the pastor, to decide whether agents for other objects than those already approved by the church, shall have liberty to present them and take public collections.

1842.   *January* 31.   Dea. N. E. Thayer, wishing to be excused from the active duties of the deaconship on account

of many and increasing infirmities—and Dea. D. Hollis pre-
ferring a similar request, and the request being deemed rea-
sonable—this day was set apart for the choice of two assistant
deacons; brethren Nathaniel Hayward and Charles Dickerman
were unanimously chosen by ballot to the office.

On the same day a "standing rule," that had been in ope-
ration for thirty years, requiring applicants for admission from
other Congregational churches to submit to examination by the
committee, in like manner as those " coming out from the
world," was formally RESCINDED ; and it was voted, that " full
letters of recommendation " from " churches with which we
are in fellowship, be received as sufficient testimonials of
christian character and standing." The *occasion* of the above
" standing rule " having passed away, when the dividing line
between Evangelical and Unitarian Congregationalists had
been fairly established and recognized, the rule had become
superfluous, and even derogatory to the character of sister
churches.

February 27. After a sermon on " the office, qualifications,
and duties of deacons," the previously elected brethren, Nathaniel Hayward and Charles Dickerman, were inducted into
office by solemn prayer, and the laying on of hands.

1854. *October* 19. Our beloved brother Dickerman, having been called away from us by death—at a special meeting
of the church, notified for the purpose, brother Elias Hayward was chosen to succeed in the office of deacon, by an
unanimous vote of the members present. After due consider-
ation, on his part,

November 14. Bro. E. Hayward was publicly inducted into office, at the close of the afternoon service, by prayer and
the laying on of hands.

1857. *June* 3. A new house of worship having been
erected in place of the former, which, in the judgment of
many, had become insufficient to accommodate the increasing
population, was this day solemnly dedicated to the service of
God agreeably to previous arrangements. Rev. Mr. Couch, of
N. Bridgewater, offered the invocation and read the scriptures;
Rev. Mr. Means, of Dorchester, read the hymn ; Rev. Mr.
Russel, of E. Randolph, offered prayer ; Rev. R. S. Storrs, Jr.,
of Brooklyn, preached the sermon ; the Pastor offered the

prayer of dedication ; Rev. Mr. Perkins, of East Braintree, gave the benediction. An overflowing congregation shared the solemnities of the occasion, and many prayers went up to God, that the glory of the latter house might exceed the glory of the former.

September 6. The communion vessels hitherto in use in this church being no longer needful here, since the generous donation of a complete set by Mrs. L. Bliss, of Boston, formerly a member of this church, were donated to the use of a feeble church in Ohio, at the suggestion of Rev. Henry M. Storrs, Cincinnati ; the few articles presented as special memorials by honored individuals being retained for continued use.

1858. *February* 25. It was voted that the standing committee be authorised, if they see fit, to draft a code of By-laws for the regulation of the action of the church in the future, and present it for adoption at the next annual meeting, or at a special meeting, duly notified, if they think proper.

1859. *January* 3. A report of " Rules and Regulations," previously agreed upon by the standing committee, agreeably to the preceding vote, was presented to the church, accepted and adopted ; and the same committee was authorized to publish it, in connexion with a revised edition of the church manual. prepared in 1829.

RULES AND REGULATIONS

FIRST CHURCH IN BRAINTREE.

I. Ordinances.

1. The Lord's Supper shall be administered, God willing, four times a year, viz. : on the first Sabbath in the several months of March, June, September, and December ; also, at such other times as the Church or Standing Committee shall elect.

2. Baptism shall be administered to the children of believing parents, on the same Sabbaths ; or, if greater convenience require, it may be administered at other times.

II. Annual Meeting.

1. The Church shall hold an annual meeting for business, on or near the first day of January of each year; when the Record of the preceding Annual Meeting shall be read, and the Divine blessing implored.

2. Two permanent Committees for the year shall be chosen, by ballot or nomination, as the Church shall direct; 1st, a committee of business, called a " Standing Committee ;" 2d, a committee for the management of the Sabbath School, called the " Sabbath School Committee."

3. These committees shall consist each of six members, beside the pastor, who shall be a member *ex officio*.

4. Other committees for special purposes may be chosen, at the discretion of the Church.

5. All these committees shall make report of their doings at the close of the year, or at any special meeting of the Church, if required ; and submit them to the action of the Church.

6. At this meeting a Treasurer shall be appointed, to take charge of the collections of the Church, and report thereon. A Clerk shall also be chosen, to record the doings of the Church, and keep them open to the inspection of members.

III. Special Meetings.

1. Special Meetings of the Church may be called at any time, when judged necessary, by the pastor, Standing Committee, or any seven members of the Church, signing their names to the call.

2. Such meetings shall be notified from the pulpit, on the Sabbath preceding ; or, if the pastor refuse so to notify them, a written notification, duly signed by seven members or more, stating the business or object of the meeting, and posted on an intervening Sabbath in the vestibule of the Meeting-house, shall be deemed a regular notice ; and the business transacted at such meeting shall be held regular and valid.

IV. Moderator.

1. In all meetings of the Church the pastor shall be the Moderator, unless he decline to serve, or refuse to discharge the duties of the office.

2. In case of the pastor's sickness, unavoidable absence, or refusal to serve, the Church may appoint a Moderator for the time being.

V. Quorum.

1. A majority of the acting members present at the regular meetings of the Church, shall form a quorum for business.

2. All business transactions shall be determined by a majority of the votes actually cast on any given question ; and any vote carried by more or less in the affirmative, shall be declared unanimous, if no negative votes be cast.

VI. Standing Committee.

1. It shall be the duty of this Committee to meet at least once in three months, and as much oftener as necessity shall require, or convenience permit. These meetings shall be open to any member of the Church wishing to profit by the deliberations of the Committee.

2. They shall examine all those offering themselves as candidates for admission to the privileges of the Church, and if satisfied of their experimental piety and doctrinal correctness, shall propound them for admission, three, or at least two weeks, previous to calling for a vote of the Church; the formal vote being taken at the close of the preparatory lecture preceding the communion. In the case of those bringing letters of dismission and recommendation from sister Churches held in fellowship, it shall suffice for the pastor to propound them, as others are propounded, and call for the vote of the Church, in the same manner; it being understood, that no member of another Church shall be received into this Church, without proper letters of dismission and recommendation.

3. Cases of discipline shall be taken up by this Committee, on complaint regularly brought before them, and made the subject of inquiry and kindly effort to convince and reclaim the offender, or to remove misapprehensions from the mind of the complainant; but no person shall be cut off from the Church, except by vote of the Church at a regular meeting.

4. This Committee shall give letters of dismission and recommendation to those removing to another place, or wishing, for *any* reasons, to connect themselves with a sister Church, if in good and regular standing at the time of making the request.

5. This Committee shall look after the spiritual interests, so far as they have the ability to do it, of such members of the Church, as, through removal or other causes, fail to commune regularly, or occasionally, at least, with this Church, and neglect other duties pledged in their covenant engagements.

VII.   Resident Members of other Churches.

Members of other Churches residing and worshipping with us, are expected, after the lapse of a year at the longest, to present letters of dismission from the Church to which they belong; and in case no satisfactory reason for further delay be assigned, they are expected to absent themselves from the communion of this Church.

VIII.   The Sabbath School Committee.

This Committee shall appoint the Superintendent and teachers of the School; determine what text-books shall be used; at what times and places the sessions shall be held; what books shall be placed in the library, and on what conditions used by the scholars; take up an annual collection for the increase of the library; and aid the active laborers in the School, by their counsels, personal influence, and cheerful efforts.

IX.   Disposal of Funds.

1.   A collection shall be taken at the close of every sacramental lecture, for defraying the expenses of the communion table.

2.   Any surplus funds remaining in the hands of the deacons, after supplying the Lord's table, shall be distributed to indigent members of the church, if such there be; otherwise, they shall be reserved in the hands of the Treasurer, till cases of want arise, or other appropriation is made by vote of the church.

X.   Discipline.

Believing that sound and wholesome discipline is essential to the peace and welfare of any church, we adopt and abide by the rules Christ has prescribed for its maintainance, in Matt. 18 c., and which are elucidated by the records of the primitive church.

We recognize two classes of offences, viz: those of a private and personal character, and those that are public, or open to the observation of all.

1. In the case of private or personal wrongs, the member aggrieved shall himself take the several steps prescribed by Christ; in the case of public offence, the Standing Committee shall take the same course; and if satisfaction be not given, the matter shall be laid before the Church at the Annual Meeting, or at a meeting specially called for the purpose.

2. If the Church approve the action of the aggrieved member, in the *first* case, or of the Standing Committee, in the *second*, a written complaint, specifying the charges preferred, and signed by the Clerk, shall be placed in the hands of the offender, with a citation from the•Church or Committee, to appear at a given time and place, and make answer to said charges.

3. If he refuse to obey the citation, after a first and second summons, he shall, if the Church so elect, be forthwith excommunicated for *contumacy*, without further reference to the truth of the charges alleged; in case he appear, and answer to the charges, and after all, is voted guilty by the Church—which shall never be done, without clear and indisputable evidence against him—he must furnish satisfactory indications of repentance to the Church, or be instantly suspended from its privileges.

4. After this suspension, the Church shall delay action only so long as they judge that duty requires; and then, in case no satisfaction be given by the offender, the Church shall proceed to vote his exclusion; and this act of exclusion, signed by the Moderator and Clerk, shall be read from the pulpit, in presence of the congregation.

XI. VOTERS IN THE CHURCH.

Every acting member of this Church has the right, and shall always share the privilege, of voting, on any and every question that comes before it for its action, unless suspended, after being found guilty of some disciplinable offence.

XII. SUSPENSION OF RULES.

None of the standing Rules and Regulations of this Church shall be suspended, except by a vote of two-thirds of the members present, at any regular meeting.

4

XIII.   RESCINDING OF RULES.

No " Standing Rule " of this Church shall be rescinded or changed, unless a written proposition, stating distinctly the proposed change, be submitted at some regular meeting; and final action shall be delayed until the next succeeding Annual Meeting.

XIV.   ADDITIONAL RULES.

Any new " Standing Rule " hereafter proposed, shall be first submitted to the " Standing Committee," or to a special committee, to be by them considered, and reported to the Church for adoption or rejection, at the next regular meeting following.

XV.   AUTHORITY OF PAST RULES.

Any Rules or Regulations heretofore adopted by this Church, and put on record, or regarded as common law, being super-seded by this Digest, shall no longer be referred to, as having authority in the proceedings of this Church.

The foregoing " Rules and Regulations," prepared by the " Standing Committee," as directed by the Church at the Annual Meeting of 1858, was read at the Annual Meeting, Jan. 3, 1859; and it was "voted, unanimously, that said Report be accepted and adopted ; and that the same Committee be authorized to publish it, in connection with the revised edition of the Church Manual."

Attest,   R. S. STORRS, *Pastor and Clerk.*

VIOLATION OF COVENANT ENGAGEMENTS.

" You covenant to attend the worship and ordinances of the Gospel with the Church, so long as God continues you in the world, and you are able to do it." ·

Upon this article in the church Covenant, the " Standing Committee " made report, at the annual meeting of the church, January 2, 1860; which was accepted unanimously:

" This Covenant your committee understand to be violated,

I. When any member of the church, resident with us, having ordinary health, and no special physical hindrance, yet abstains from the regular commemoration of the death of Christ, in the way of his appointment. If any brother or sister be offended by the supposed or real misconduct of any member of the church, his duty is plain, to go directly to the offender, and obtain satisfaction in the mode prescribed by the Savior, Matt. 18th, and not to cut himself off from the communion of the whole church with her Lord and Master, and thereby grieve all the brethren. Offences will come; but they often originate in misapprehensions, which a calm and fraternal interchange of thought would remove; and, it is injurious to any brother to condemn him, before giving him an opportunity to explain himself; and still more injurious to the whole church to condemn it as a body, for the real or supposed misconduct of an individual. No offence, real or imaginary, is ever removed by the commission of another offence."

Authority sustaining these views of the Committee.

Nearly two hundred years ago " the Cambridge Association " discussed the question:

" What is the duty of the church to persons, who upon private prejudices, withdraw from the communion of it?"

" The following propositions were agreed upon," and ever

since have been accepted by the churches, as true and scriptural bases of action :

"1.   Persons that have taken up any private prejudice against any in the communion of the church whereto they do belong, are directed by the commandment of the Lord Jesus Christ, and are engaged by the covenant of watchfulness, to endeavor the repentance of the persons under supposed offence, by a personal application.

"2.   They, that upon offence taken, do neglect this way of proceeding, are guilty of sin against the Lord's commandment, and their own covenant; and by their withdrawing from the table of the Lord, their sin is aggravated.

"3.   The withdrawing of persons thus irregularly from the communion of the church at the Lord's table, does carry a hard and high imputation upon the church itself, which adds more of a fault unto so sinful a schism.

"4.   If the person that hath been offended hath done his duty, and either the pastor do refuse to lay the matter before the church, for the insignificancy of it, or the church upon hearing of it, do pronounce itself satisfied, the person is obliged still to continue his communion with the church, until a council of churches declare the contrary.

"5.   Such a sinful separation from the communion of the church, being a moral evil, the scandal is to be, by the discipline of the church, proceeded against, as other censurable scandals.   The pastor, upon observation of the sin, is to send for the person withdrawing, [or otherwise see him,] and instruct, and convince, and admonish him ; and, upon contumacious obstinacy, the church is to deal with him, as one unruly and walking disorderly.

"6.   Nevertheless, compassion towards the ignorant, or injured, is very much to determine the more or less vigor wherewith such offences are to be prosecuted."

Upham's Ratio Disciplinæ.   Sec. 210.

II.   On the withdrawal of pecuniary support from the worship and ordinances of the Gospel — a further and obvious violation of covenant — the same Committee report, that

1.   "Every church-member has a right, so long as in good and regular standing, to claim letters of dismission to a sister church, if, for reasons satisfactory to himself, he can better be edified by worship with said sister church than his own.   But,

2. "The public worship of God — the preaching of the Gospel, and the observance of the sacraments — the Lord's Supper and Baptism, are divine ordinances — not a human device; nor are they sustained by any other law · than the law of Christ, though civil law commend and encourage them.

3. "*Whoever* withholds his presence and pecuniary aid, from all, or either of these ordinances, violates the law of Christ; and, if a member of the church, he violates covenant obligations also; and the church is bound by *her* engagements, to "watch over him, with all tenderness and fidelity," endeavoring to remove his misapprehensions, — and in failure of this, to adopt with him the line of conduct prescribed by Christ, as an offender against the law of his kingdom."

4. "However just and equitable is "the law of the land," that each individual pay, in proportion to the property of which God has made him the steward, your Committee do not insist on this rule of contribution as fixed and invariable, but leave it to the conscience and heart of each individual, in the sight of God, to determine how much the divine law of equity requires him to contribute to the honor of that Saviour who gave his LIFE for the ransom of the church, and the individual believer.

By order of the Standing Committee.

R. S. STORRS, *Pastor and Clerk*.

www.ingramcontent.com/pod-product-compliance
Lightning Source LLC
Chambersburg PA
CBHW032140080426
42733CB00008B/1139